Suzuki®

BASS SCHOOL

Volume 3
Piano Accompaniment
Revised Edition

AMPV: 1.00

© 2015, 2004, 1996 Dr. Shinichi Suzuki
Sole publisher for the entire world except Japan:
Summy-Birchard, Inc.
Exclusive print rights administered by Alfred Music Publishing Co., Inc.
All rights reserved   Printed in USA

ISBN-10: 0-87487-377-0
ISBN-13: 978-0-87487-377-1

INTRODUCTION

FOR THE STUDENT: This material is part of the worldwide Suzuki Method® of teaching. The companion recording should be used along with this publication. In addition, there are bass part books that go along with this material.

FOR THE TEACHER: In order to be an effective Suzuki teacher, ongoing education is encouraged. Each regional Suzuki association provides teacher development for its membership via conferences, institutes, short-term and long-term programs. In order to remain current, you are encouraged to become a member of your regional Suzuki association, and, if not already included, the International Suzuki Association.

FOR THE PARENT: Credentials are essential for any Suzuki teacher you choose. We recommend you ask your teacher for his or her credentials, especially those related to training in the Suzuki Method®. The Suzuki Method® experience should foster a positive relationship among the teacher, parent and child. Choosing the right teacher is of utmost importance.

To obtain more information about the Suzuki Association in your region, please contact:

International Suzuki Association
www.internationalsuzuki.org

CONTENTS

1
Moon Over the Ruined Castle

Rentaro Taki

2
Minuet No. 2

J.S. Bach

3
Ode to Joy

L. van Beethoven

4
Andantino

S. Suzuki

5
Trilling Waltz

Virginia Dixon

6

Sweet Georgia Brown

B. Bernie, M. Pinkard
K. Casey
Arranged by Daniel Swaim

*Bar and lift the fourth finger after playing pizzicato. Play pizzicato with the right thumb at the lower end of the fingerboard for this double-stop chord.

0377S

This page has been left blank intentionally to facilitate page turns.

7

Large from the "New World Symphony"

A. Dvórak

8
Bourree

G.F. Handel

9
Gavotte

F.J. Gossec

0377S

10

So What

M. Davis
Arranged by Daniel Swaim

11
A Gaelic Melody

Chester Minkler

12

L' Elephant
from Le Carnaval des Animaux

C. Saint-Saens

13
Scherzo

C. Webster

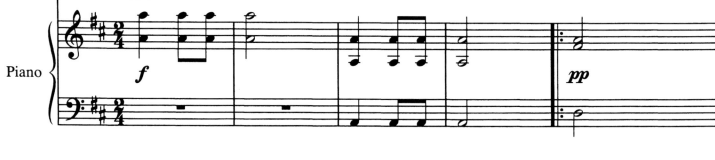

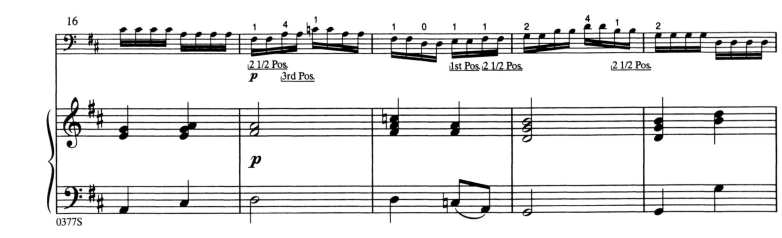

0377S

0377S